David:

"Heaven's Addition"

A testimony of
strength that only
God can provide.

By

**Dad:
Marcus W. Turner**

This book was printed in the United States of America.
To order additional copies of this book contact:

For Worthwhile Books Publications
Columbus, Ohio
ISBN 9798649442954 Soft cover| Grief | Sorrow |Trauma

TABLE OF CONTENTS

DEDICATION

This book is dedicated to The Lord Jesus Christ, our all omnipotent God, his Grace that provided me strength and Peace of Eternity. To David, my son, whom I know now is ever mindful of his loved ones and is close by with his strength and courage to inspire us. To my spouse Iris, who has loved me through this difficult time. To every soul that receives inspiration from this testimony.

"The Lord bless you and keep you; the Lord make his face shine upon you, and be gracious to you; the Lord lift up his countenance upon you, and give you peace."

Numbers 6:24-26
(KJV)

DAVID:

"HEAVEN'S ADDITION"

INTRODUCTION

I have never kept journals. I have never had a diary.

I am not an English major, nor do I possess any special literary skills. Writing a book has never been a task I thought I would undertake. Even now as I pen this, I have no specific outline to follow, nor do I have any certainty it will be accomplished. That statement is not in any form negative. It would be appropriate to just say, "I don't know what I am doing."

I only know this: I have a testimony that I do believe, with everything within me, can and will help some, inspire someone, or maybe even help draw some — you? — closer to God.

The events I envision telling, in the context of a book, are events that have occurred, engulfed, and surrounded my life in the months, and now past a year, after losing my youngest son, David, from this earthly life granted us.

If you are one who believes in the supernatural power of God, I hope and pray this book strengthens you. If you are totally averse to such belief, maybe you shouldn't waste your time reading. I do not have any thoughts of writing this book in an to attempt to convert anyone nor to debate anyone's belief system.

What I write happened in my life.

These are real exact experiences that came to me, occurred with me, as I yearned for help from what I know to be a living God.

Many of the occurrences transpired as I reached a point of total desperation. One thing became commonplace for me: with each event in my life, I became more and more a believer and more convinced that God is more than able to perform all we seek and need. The key is He knows when and what is best.

I am not certain how to bring the multiple elements of a book together: a preface, the chapters, how much of my life to explain to better illustrate the desperation I found in myself when David went to be with the Lord. So why am I attempting this now? I am 100% convinced that in some way I am to share God's gifts and blessings He has given me. While I have grown to better understand that God does love us so much and desires to comfort our griefs and sorrows, I do not believe that all He has done for me was just for me. I am obligated and charged to testify and to share. This book is to that end.

This book is meant to be about God's miracles, about God's visitations in my life to comfort, heal, and strengthen me while losing the earthly fellowship I had with my son.

However, I feel that it will have more impact and meaning if it starts with a brief overview of my life. This is not an autobiography and falls far short of a comprehensive picture into my personal life; but the basis, the groundwork of my up-bringing, and the belief system instilled in me are consequently what predicated my dispositions and thoughts leading up to David going home to the Lord.

The experiences God has graciously provided me to get me through have been so many, and I know they would slip from my short memory as time goes on.

Focusing on these experiences in moments of depressing relapses of sorrow provides spiritual relief. So, I began writing them down in a scratch notebook. Some days I dated them; others, in my rush to pen them down, I overlooked dating. I often referred to that notebook as "David's Book." That may well end up being the title.

May God anoint and bless this effort.
Marcus

CHAPTER ONE

LIFE'S PATH

I was born to Jasper "Pete" and Marie Turner on December 10, 1954 in Durham, NC. I was the third of five children. I was that middle child with two older sisters and two younger brothers.

I can't say we were the poorest, as we had a house to live in, food on the table, clothing, and an automobile. However, financially, we were certainly at the lower end of the success ladder. Dad was a welder, a WWII veteran who left school in the third grade. His family was poor, and he grew up working. Mom graduated high school and attended a technical school for a while.

I remember well our first home where the family lived when I was born until I was age six. Our home had four rooms - two bedrooms and a living area that joined a small kitchen and dining area.

We had one small bathroom. My oldest sister, Naomi, was eight years older than I. My other sister, Phyllis, is three years older than I. Three years after I came my brother Tony, and then Roby, my youngest brother, came five years later.

Dad worked many long hours, days and nights. I remember the one-hundred-hour work week stories. Mom was the stay at home mom. She took care of the home in every way. We always ate at home, no dining out. She made most of the clothes she and my sisters wore and did all the altering and seamstress work for mine. I guess she was our personal tailor.

I was raised to go to church every time the doors were open. Mom and all the children were always in church. Dad did not usually go. He went a few times, but that was not the norm.

The doctrine of the church we were raised in would be best described as Pentecostal Holiness. By the standards taught, Mom was a faithful steward. Dad, well, he was considered a sinner. Dad smoked cigarettes, drank alcohol excessively, cursed sometimes, and hung out with other sinners, "people of the world."

Our church taught us that many things we experience or see in life were not acceptable before God; indeed, we would be sinners to participate, and of course sinners go to Hell. The standards I refer to were things such as: I could not wear shorts, and the ladies, my sisters, could not wear dresses that showed the knees. Makeup and jewelry were not allowed. Activities that seem normal to most, such as going to the movies, attending ballgames, being on a sports team, attending county or state fairs, concerts of music that wasn't spiritual or Gospel, and listening to any kind of music not spiritual or gospel, were not allowed. We were sinners and Hell-bound if we did those things. If the ladies cut their hair or wore slacks, or if any alcohol was consumed, we were sinners and would go to Hell.

It is not the purpose of this book to explain the Biblical writings used to support the aforementioned beliefs. It is not the purpose of this book to break out what I may or may not still believe about the standards of the Christian life.

As stated earlier, I am just showing the state of my mind as a child and how it progressed as I became a teenager, a young adult, and to my current state. I'm describing what I was taught from a child about what it took to be a Christian and not die and go to Hell, and how I grew from that to the belief system I have now and had when David left us.

I understood early how much our mother loved us and all she would endure to provide for us and help ensure that God saved us, and we would go to Heaven. My mom believed all she taught us and dedicated her life to providing for us and teaching us God's way. Was there some error there? I believe so. Was it born of love and desire for us to be saved? I know so.

In the breakout times in my life, I realized the traditions taught carried some human interpretations of God's laws and expectations of us. These times revealed a lot to me, but they also presented challenges.

How should I lead my children in these areas? Just like my mom, I must instruct my children correctly with God's laws and requirements.

My views on Christian life today are certainly different in many ways than those taught me as a child; however, I do believe God expects us to live a holy life before Him and hold up a standard, as opposed to the view that we should be accepting of all lifestyles as personal choice and equally acceptable to God.

I believe in a Heaven and a Hell. That has not changed with me. If your belief system tells you that this life is it or it tells you that all go to a glorious place regardless of the life you live on earth, then as I said before, don't waste your time reading this book.

In these pages, I will share real experiences the God of the Heavens and Earth gave me. These are not dreaming, not moments of trance craziness, but are life-saving, God-loving visitations to reveal to me that God loves me. God knows my pain, and He cares. He has and continues to make a way for me to get through to eternity, to arrive there with my faith and salvation intact, and yes, to feel the chest of my son hug me again!

One other belief drilled into me all of my childhood, teens and adulthood is that one must believe the way the church taught the Scripture.

In order to be saved, one must be baptized a particular way and one must receive the gift of the Holy Ghost a certain way.

Once more I will state, I am not taking this space to explain if or how I believe doctrine today. I am setting up the belief system instilled in me and the consequent desperation I felt to know that David was safe with God.

Thank God I have learned scripturally that to whom much is known, much is required, little known, little required.

God has taken care of me. My life has been preserved for His purposes if I but follow. I have lost nothing in this life that He will not restore many times over in eternity, and my love for God grows every day.

Through my childhood and teenage years and as a young adult, I gave my life to God the way I was taught. I was faithful in every way.

I wanted to go to Heaven. Questions finally began to arise in my heart and mind in my mid-teens. The answers were always that this was the life required of me. The late teens began to present more mounting issues and questions, but nothing was worth losing my soul.

My twenties brought about marriage. My spouse had been taught the same as I, religiously.

At the birth of my first son, Daniel, reality was catching up with me. I was beginning to question and lose faith in the leadership of our assembly.

This questioning rocked some of the beliefs and standards drilled into me all of my life.

My second son, David, was born two years after

Daniel. Within a year, my wife and I separated. That also brought a separation from the church. Separation and divorce were sin.

I must express again, these writings are not meant to dwell on what I was taught, believed and lived. My words are to paint the vivid picture of my state of mind, desperation, and need for God the day David went to be near God's presence.

There was no separation or divorce of my sons when Linda and I split. Fortunately, she and I never needed divorce court. Our children's love and stability were first for us. They lived with her primarily, but I kept them most weekends and visited many times during the week as work responsibilities allowed.

One big consequence of this lifestyle was my children were not in church many times. Linda left the church a few years later. I was unsettled as to what was truly a Christian life. What was truth or error in what I was taught? How do I teach my children and how do I explain to them a Christian life? Having realized in my adulthood that I learned some good Christian practices but also some things that were not right, I questioned. What is right? What is wrong? One realizes how daunting a responsibility it is to teach your children God's way, the right way. Did I really even know?

By God's grace we raised two good boys.

They weren't restricted to some standards we were taught but were taught to live a good life and how they should treat others. They were exposed to the belief that God must live in you, but they weren't taught the exact way we were taught regarding the Holy Ghost.

CHAPTER TWO

TRAGEDIES

I was thirty-nine years of age when I lost my dad. I was recovering from a major auto accident, still in a halo brace as a result of a broken neck. EMS reported at the accident scene that I would be dead-on-arrival (DOA) or paralyzed from the neck down. God was gracious in leading me to a full recovery.

While my dad was a mostly absent parent, and life with a Christian mom and an often-drunk husband wasn't at all pleasant many times, I loved Dad. Seeing him go and experiencing the passing of an immediate family member was so difficult for me, though I do feel God had somewhat prepared me for that day. The last few years had been pleasant and loving ones, but the years of alcohol and tobacco abuse had resulted in heart and other chronic conditions. I heard Dad refer to dying many times. I didn't feel Dad would live much longer.

My oldest sister, Naomi, is eight years older than I. Growing up, she was a second mom. She remained so supportive and such a strong sister to me in my young adult life. She was the organist in our church for forty years, and I led and directed much of the spiritual singing.

Her support there as the organist and as my second mom figure held my faith together many times.

Naomi was working a part-time job in a local store in Durham, NC and was murdered during a robbery there. That horrific event and the subsequent tragedies in my life over the next several years would leave me in a mental and emotional turmoil difficult to describe.

Naomi's only child, Joanna, my first niece, would pass on less than two years later. Her mother meant the world to her. Intense grieving over losing her mom, coupled with abuse of the multiple anxiety and depression medications she used for relief, took her life.

Joanna was very special. Losing her held tremendous pain for me.

A year or so later, we would lose Naomi's husband, Harold, to cancer. The grief he endured losing his wife and only daughter left him little strength to fight the cancer.

For me, saying goodbye to Naomi and her entire family so tragically was very painful and long-lasting.

My brother Tony had been through some rough times over the past few years in his life. All the family had been supporting him in various ways. He and I grew up only three years apart in age and very close.

I played an integral part in Tony's life, assisting with some of his challenges. He was fifty-six, and over the course of the last two months, his life had finally changed for the better. I am thankful I had assisted.

Then I received a phone call. He had been hit on his bicycle and killed. It was a hit and run; the driver was never found. Only two years had passed since Naomi had left us, followed by her family.

Suffice to say, I felt, "Lord, I can't take anymore!"

At ninety-one, Mom was very healthy and had a strong heart.

She often said she would live to be one hundred. I believed the doctors thought so as well. But those few years were very hard on her, obviously. Losing a daughter, who was a right hand to her, losing a grand-daughter and son-in-law, and now a son took its toll on her physically; and I am convinced it wore on her mental health, as well. In summary, six months before Mom passed, no one ever thought she would leave any time soon. Even though her last six months showed some frailty, her passing so quickly was not expected.

These family tragedies, briefly rehearsed, are done so as to open a window into my soul to view the emotional stress bound inside when David was called home to God's presence.

The highway to my office included a stretch on the 540 loops around Raleigh, NC. In those slow travel times, I often meditated in silent prayer to God. I remember praying, more than once, for the safety and long life of my sons and spouse. I remember expressing to the Lord that I could never make it if anything happened to my sons. "Please, Lord, protect them."

It was on that same stretch of highway that I received a call that David was not at work in the office; he was approaching an hour late. He was not answering the telephone. I called Linda, his mom, to see if she had heard from David. She had not, and she immediately left her home to go check on him.

This morning I was actually driving to Durham to take care of some final business for my mom who had passed on just seven days before. I detoured to David's apartment to check on him.

Linda got to David's apartment first. She lived in Durham, only ten minutes from his home. I lived in Raleigh, a half hour away.

Linda's call came to me. She was so upset, crying. David had gone to be with the Lord.

[To get off track for a moment, it has been a couple of weeks since I have made entries or written anything into these writings.

The last section, of driving into Durham when I received the call, broke me down so emotionally that I had to lay the pen down.

Setting the stage and painting the picture of that morning is necessary to tell the story, but I wasn't emotionally prepared. The last couple of weeks, I doubted that I could continue. Writing this book... well, I had not anticipated the sorrow and pain it would open up and I would have to relive. However, again, God is with me.

I am very anxious to get to God's miraculous events in my life that helped me and, I trust, will help some of you reading. They bring some sorrow rehearsing, but so much more joy. The book is meant to express God's miracles and a testimony for others; but for the writing of it, I need God's grace again.]

When Linda told me over the telephone, screaming and crying, "David is gone," my life stopped. My whole world ceased. "I cannot bear this."

I got to David's apartment. Law enforcement was there. My son Daniel, Linda, and others were there. As I approached the apartment door, police stopped me. I completely broke down. "It's my son! I have to go in; you cannot hold me." I was not going to let that happen. I had to see my son.

They allowed me to go in, but they held on to me, restricting me. They only allowed me to the bedroom doorway.

I fell to the floor as I saw David sitting on the floor, bent over from the waist, his upper body to his legs. His finished dinner from the evening before was at his feet. I crawled and reached to touch him as they held me back. My boy, my son, my David was gone.

[Writing this part is extremely painful. I realize now why I have had to wait this long to again pick up the pen and relive the next horrible hours, trying to be there for David's brother Daniel; my heart breaking for Linda and for my wife, Iris, David's step-mom. My world was destroyed.

While I must describe my desperation, my real purpose is to share God's grace, praying that it helps others. I now know how much more it is my responsibility to do so. Despite these painful entries, I know it's God's will for me to do this.]

That afternoon, at home in Raleigh, I went for a long walk.

Much of my walk was through the woods. I had to find an altar. The evening passed in total horrific pain, anguish, and much prayer.

The next morning, God's special visitations in my life began.

Many days into my life with David gone to be with the Lord, I realized that I needed to write down God's gifts and the visitation experiences He provided me. The first thing I wrote was somewhat of a prelude:

"In times of pain and desires to know David is in God's presence and with joy and peace, God gave me the following experiences and promises."

CHAPTER THREE

GOD'S PROMISE

August 9, 2017

The next morning, I went again to a wooded area and fell on my knees. I prayed. I begged God for peace.

"Lord, David was never given a physical water baptism. He wasn't taught this doctrine or that rule. He didn't belong to a church. God, he did all he knew. He was a good man."

I can rehearse how his life demonstrated his love for people, especially for children. Often what he did for others was to his own impoverishment and showed his unselfishness. He loved people. He acted on and lived all that he knew. I begged God for assurance that David is safe in heaven.

"God help me," I even said in my heart, "if David isn't there, Lord, I don't want to go."

Behind that heart thought, I ask for God's mercy. I didn't want to blaspheme God, but I hurt so much. People telling me that David is in Heaven wasn't enough. Words of just comfort weren't enough. Only God knew, and I needed God to tell me. I had to have that.

"God, I have to know. I cannot live without that peace."

Still on my knees praying to the Lord, my cell phone rang. It was Linda: "I want to check on you." I unloaded the travail of my soul. I told her, "I have to know, from God, that David is in Heaven with our Lord." Linda immediately said to me, "Remember the video David sent you?" "What video?"
She said, "David sent you a video Saturday night. It was late at night. Didn't you get it?" (This was the Saturday evening before David left us on Monday night.)

I exclaimed to Linda, "I had forgotten! Yes, he sent me something on YouTube; it was almost 1:00 AM. I heard my cell phone chime that I had a message." Sleepy and groggy, I had thought it was a comedic standup routine by someone I wasn't familiar with. I didn't completely watch it. I actually viewed very little at that time. I was sleepy and thought I would watch it in the morning and went back to bed.

Sadly, I forgot the next morning.

There in the woods, after I hung up with Linda, I opened and viewed the video David sent me entitled "A Shadow of a Doubt" by Joseph Solomon.
The summary:

Joseph Solomon rehearsed, "I remember my little niece telling me she learned about Jesus today." She knew it was true because Mommy said so.

He envied his niece, because she had no doubts, while his entire belief system had doubts, and had for so long. "I've had lots of questions, but not enough answers. I've prayed to God every night to help me." He watched his grandmother pass. While worried, she assured that she knew who she belonged to. He was so happy for her and wished somehow his grandmother could pass that faith to him. He sleeps but never rests. He has grown so tired. He longs to see Jesus. He doesn't question God, but he has lots of questions. "Please, God, don't leave me!"

The answer came. "Have your questions, but believe God's Word. Before you doubt God, doubt your doubts. They are as empty as the tomb I walked from. My love will drive out this fear. I am there for you; I'm yours; you are Mine. Until death brings us closer, you are Mine, and I am yours, I promise."

I hope you can stop now - if not, then later- and view this video.

You should be able to locate it on youtube.com. Search "A Shadow of a Doubt," by Joseph Solomon. It is about seven minutes in length. As I had begged God in prayer that morning in the woods, praying desperately for God's assurance of David being with the Lord, only minutes, maybe seconds, passed when Linda called me and shared this video. This video was so direct: God stating, "Until death brings us together, you are Mine, and I am yours!"

Linda told me before she hung up and I viewed the video in its entirety, "David told me, 'Mom, this video is so me.'"

God answered my prayer in the woods that morning. It wasn't an analogy or just some good thought. It was a direct message from God through David for me this morning. It was sent to me even before David left, but received at God's time.

"Thank you, Lord!"

The video David sent to me two days before leaving was the first of many experiences to come, by the grace of God. His love is so strong, so far reaching, and has saved my soul and preserved my life here for His purposes.

The remainder of this book will be about God's gifts to me. I pray all of you who read will become more convinced that if we but ask and believe, God will answer.

CHAPTER FOUR

GOD'S VISITATIONS

Not dated

Linda called me. We shared God's gifts for strength. She had been crying. The first few days after David leaving, most days were spent crying. She called to tell me, "Marcus, it was so real. It wasn't audible that others would have heard, but it was so real. I heard David say to me, 'Mom, stop crying. I'm alright.'" Linda told me she wasn't asking God for anything; she was just crying uncontrollably, and she heard David speak.

I know of a certainty that God speaks to the heart. I know God allows those that have gone on before us to speak to us as well. I am reminded of the Apostle Paul: he heard Jesus Christ speak to him from the heavens. Those all around him saw the light, but only Paul heard.

This incident God blessed Linda with, and me with hearing about it, may sound simple to many. Some may say or think that it was just contrived by the mind. I know without any doubt the Lord sends answers, blessings, and comfort when we most need them.

There will be more of these simple interventions God blessed me with as these writings continue.

I won't analyze them all. Simply put, they are little nuggets God has given me all along this way to comfort and strengthen. God can live within you, if you but ask and believe. He also will talk to you and lead you, if you be still and listen.

We all have had songs ring in our heads, something catchy, heard recently or something heard many times, also usually recently.

As a song leader in church for many years and as a singer of Gospel music, I learned hundreds of songs. Having been away from that position for almost 30 years, many of them were no longer in my recent memory. To have a song just start ringing in my head and finding myself singing it, well, it was quite a spiritual uplift!

On this particular grieving morning, as I stepped into the shower, my heart ached with pain. Tears flowed. Suddenly, as if the music just started, I began singing.

"And the toils of this life will seem nothing, when I get to the end of the way.
And the toils of this life will seem nothing, when I get to the end of my way."

I hadn't heard this song in decades, and the words were merely a distant memory. Realizing the Lord had brought the song to my memory was such a comfort of His love and care for my pain. I was praying;

I was crying. I just started singing the song out loud. I hope all my readers can feel how powerful this was. God, the God and Lord of the heavens, set my heart and soul singing with the most fitting song from decades past.

"Jesus Christ the same yesterday, today, and forever." Hebrews 13:8

I was sitting on the bench I have in a natural area of landscape, to the right front side of our home. I often sit there to read, think, pray, and listen to music. This particular day, I was pondering my career and the possible financial needs of my family.

Having been a believer of using life insurance to secure financial protection for my family should I pass on before our savings are sufficient, on this day I was considering the need to purchase some additional coverage. My evaluations always include the possible needs of our family business, my spouse, my adult sons, and my dependent elderly mother.

As I considered these needs that I would desire to be allotted for, I felt these words speak into my heart: "You have enough life insurance."

The feeling was as strong as if it were audible. I have had these experiences before, and I know them to be God speaking to me.

The message I felt from God dispelled my concerns that were based on mathematical calculations. I made those calculations considering that I would likely live to be a certain age. I guessed God was telling me that I wasn't going to live longer than the coverage I had would suffice. I accepted the message for two reasons.

I felt the words as real as if audible. And God knows the age I will leave this life.

Just as I reconciled these thoughts, additional words came to me: "Lessen your travels and travel plans. The family needs you this year."

My business takes me out-of-state often during our peak season, February-August. My mom, age 91, needed more and more daily care. I felt this was the reason God must be sending me these messages. I honestly, for the first time, felt I would lose my mom this year. Her health was strong. Her arthritis and pain necessitated more mobile care, but again her vital organs and overall health was fine.

I firmly believed at the time that God was beginning to prepare me for her passing. Thus, the messages about life insurance and staying home close to the family this year. Mom did need me close for multiple reasons.

Obviously, God knew the future of my son David as well. I heeded the message. I greatly reduced my travels that spring and summer. While I did not see my mom and son every day, nor every week, I was there. I was available.

The days ahead would prove to me, and greater reveal to me, that God knows our path before it approaches. He also makes a way for us to get through. He prepares us if we put our faith in him. I am so thankful and praise Him, and just marvel at God's grace and goodness.

As I sat on my bench that day, He was near me and preparing me. With my schedule reduced for traveling, I was more in contact with David over the coming months, and we indeed played more golf together. Mom was always a daily telephone contact, and I could be more handson. God knew in His foreknowledge, and made a way for me.

My wife Iris, David's stepmom, saw David almost every day during the work week. David worked in our office for about five years. Iris is our office administrator and my partner in the business. Needless to say, David's passing has been hard on her as well.

The following may not seem much to some, but it was a blessing to her. One morning, she told me she had a dream the night before. The family was sitting in a restaurant. David was sitting beside me, and Iris was standing behind David at the table. In an instant, David appeared behind Iris and whispered something in her ear. Iris said that she did not know what David said.

The dream wasn't a detailed event. We can't say the exact meaning. However, at the time she shared it with me, I knew God was intervening in my life and beginning to further provide me peace and comfort.

One particular morning, feeling emotional and stressed in my soul, I fell on my knees in the shower crying. In a brief moment, the words rang in my ears, "You can't bring him back, but you can go to him someday because of the grace of God."

That message was as real in my ears as the previous message I heard when sitting out in my front yard.

It is important to note this event this morning in the shower - God's words to me - because a later experience will confirm it.

Some of the events I describe may not seem as supernatural as others, but they are as real to me as some of the more vivid ones. I have learned that God knows my heart and my every thought. He answers our prayers, even before we pray sometimes.

These message visitations He has blessed me with are strengthening and restoring my soul. I am reminded, "God is a spirit, and they that worship Him must worship Him in spirit and in truth." (John 4:24)

I couldn't sleep, day or night. Every night I would check the clock hourly, all night long.

This evening as I sat in tremendous sorrow, I felt God's presence strongly. I began remembering the numerous blessings God had provided me: Linda calling me about the video David sent, the song God reminded me of in the shower, the experience on the bench in my front yard, Iris's dream, God speaking to me in the shower. In that instant, I felt God quicken my spirit and revive me.

I was reminded that Satan will try to steal our blessings and assurances, but God gave me His promise. As I felt God's presence, I claimed:

"I will not be defeated."

"I will live the life God presents me and put Him first in my life."

"I shall go to God's presence and hug my son again."

These little quickening's, what I know to be God stepping in with spiritual comfort, are as miraculous to me as the Lord raising the dead or healing the sick. They are personal and endearing to my soul. So many of them happen when I am not even asking. His Scriptures teach us that He knows the desires of our heart, and He knows what we need. If our heart is right with God, He will be there for us, even before we ask.

Back in the 1980s, I met three gentlemen, my brothers in the Lord. They were a singing group known as the Younce Brothers and Louie Blevins. They sang spiritual songs, and Lynual Younce wrote many of their songs.

Nine days since David went to that heavenly home.

My heart ached daily, all day.

I sat on my front yard bench and began scrolling through songs of inspiration on YouTube on my smart phone. Without specifically looking for the Younce Brothers, I came across Lynual Younce performing alone in a church he was visiting. The recording was an hour and a half long, and Lynual was talking at the beginning. Not knowing how long he would speak; I randomly scrolled the tab ahead to the 13- 14 minute mark and hit the play button. I'd take time for his testimony later; I wanted to hear a song right now. I hit play at that random mark, and he was just about to begin a song, exactly at the beginning. The song is titled, "All is Well."

The words of the song spoke of the Shunamite woman in the Bible. The song/story tells of her working in the field and her son dying. The prophet Elijah passed by and asked how her son was? Her reply: "All is well."

The song goes on to state how that today's church may be somewhat dismayed by the Lord not yet having returned to earth and by the church going through the greatest battle ever fought. I felt in my spirit God was having me put David in this song. How I was hurt and dismayed by David's passing. It is indeed the greatest battle I have ever fought. As the song also stated, "Things have not worked out as we thought, but all is well!" There are probably hundreds of songs Lynual sings. I wasn't looking for this song. I reemphasize, I fast forwarded the scroll bar and stopped randomly right on the beginning of this song, in a live performance about which I had known nothing. There is nothing coincidental about what just happened to me. The Lord is so mindful of us and our needs, when we lean on Him, when we ask believing. Even when we are asking within our spirit and not aloud, He is there. The Lord knows our need and is indeed a provider to those that diligently seek Him. The comfort the Lord has provided me, that I am now writing about, all means so much to me. However, except in those moments of reflecting on God's given experiences, the grief comes back. The Lord had already done enough for me to know with assurance that David was saved, safe in God's presence; however, the pain of losing him remains so strong. Things have not worked out as I had thought. I am fighting the greatest battle I have ever fought. David is with the Lord and all is well.

All is well.

The next day I was still focused on God's blessings and assurances from the day before. I felt led to try and contact Louie Blevins. It had been 30 years since I had seen and spoken with him. I didn't at all know how to contact him. I had heard from others the name of the church he attended in Tennessee. I looked up that church's telephone number and took a chance, calling to see if he was known there. The gentleman who answered at the church verified that Louie attended there and said he would pass my name and number on to him when he saw him again.

Only minutes passed when Brother Louie called me. The church had not contacted him. Just minutes after I called the church, Louie happened to call the church in an unrelated matter. They passed my message and contact info on to him.

This was not coincidence. This timing was so God-directed.

In that conversation when Louie called me, he stated, "If you ever were God's, you still are! So is David." Brother Louie, from that day, has been such a strength for me. He is truly a blessing from the Lord in my life.

I am growing in the knowledge that the Lord is near me every day. He is here to get me through. I must lean on Him.

Later in the evening, I came across a statement by Wintley Phipps. In his statement, he uses the term crucible. (Crucible: a situation of severe trial; or one in which elements interact, leading to the creation of something new - "baking unit.) His statement was, "It is in the quiet crucible of your personal private sufferings that your noblest dreams are born, and God's greatest gifts are given in compensation of what you have been through."

If you don't have the spiritual, the natural will kill you. The natural can never kill the spiritual.

Every day we live for the natural. The natural is gone in an instant. We better be living for the spiritual first. Enjoy the natural, live for the spiritual!

Many experiences the Lord has blessed me with are simple to explain and don't require backstory. The Lord has granted me so many divine experiences, to not only help me persevere with life but also to constantly be assured that David is in Heaven, saved by the grace of our Lord Jesus Christ. Yet, with all of the divine experiences, still I find myself weak and falling into deep sorrow. In those times, God appears, such as this morning.

Taking an early morning shower, the pain and sorrow engulfed me, and the tears flowed. As vividly as if audible, these words over- shadowed me:

"These are the sorrows sin brought to us, but the blood of Jesus Christ gives us eternal life. David didn't want to leave us now, but he would never choose to leave the joys of the Lord if given the option."

I did not imagine these words. By the grace of God, He speaks to us in our hour of need. I felt the Lord's presence; the words flowed in my mind and heart and provided such peace.

David worked with us in our agency office for five years. He was the spice of the atmosphere and was loved by all.

Gailya, one of Iris's assistants, was at her desk when I walked in this morning. She loved David very much. It was quite apparent that David was very caring of her as well. David had often said things to me that revealed his concern for her wellbeing and at times was even protective. She was someone he could talk to, and Gailya was always concerned about David and his happiness.

Like so many, Gailya hurt. For several weeks, it was difficult for her to perform at work. I stopped by her office area and shared the words of comfort and peace the Lord had provided me the mornings before.

Anxiously speaking, she said, "Mr. Turner, I have to tell you. It happened to me. I was sitting here at my desk and couldn't help but cry." Excitedly, she said, "Mr. Tuner, I heard David say, 'I'm alright.' It was so real! I could hear him say, 'Gailya, I'm all right.'" She was so joyous as she related this experience.

I remember these were the exact words Linda heard David say to her in a similar moment. But Gailya and Linda don't even know each other!

The next moments found me in my office reliving conversations I had with David.

Things I didn't think a whole lot about at the time came to mind. As I sat in my office, I remembered a particular morning when David and I were at his desk. He had something on his mind. He commented, "Dad, have you ever researched the origin of the term -(-----)?"

He whispered a profane term in my ear. I never use the foul term; however, David was serious.

It's not uncommon to hear the phrase in cussing language, and something caused David to one day research its origin. He explained how bad the origin was and what it really meant. He then said, "Dad, I could never use that term; it is so bad." I know the Lord purified David's heart.

This morning, I also remember sitting in David's apartment, counseling a little with him only a couple of months or so before the Lord took him home. David was asking for some advice. Not always having the answers, as well as desiring to be a spiritual influence on David, I remember telling him, "Son, pray. If you pray believing, God will lead you."

His response was immediate. "I do." I knew in that moment my son looked to God for answers in his life. My heart swelled with peace that day in his home. This morning as I reflected, I realized God was making me aware that David was, and is, His.

In recalling these little moments David and I shared, God was reminding me, "David is mine."

He lived all that he knew about how to live for the Lord, and David is safe with Him. Those moments with David provide me with the strength that I need now.

I am almost ashamed at how many blessings and assurances I have been given and that are continually provided by God. And yet the sorrow overshadows me so easily, and the tears flow. I have certainly learned that God's children can be a needy people.

This morning I determined to attempt to go play golf alone. David was my golfing buddy probably 75% of the time I played. I seriously wondered if I would ever be able to play again. This morning I felt I wanted to go and play alone - with David in spirit. I picked a day and a time I felt the course would be fairly empty. It worked out that way, and each hole I felt I could take my time.

By the time I reached the tee box on the fourth hole, my sorrow was overwhelming. I literally fell on my knees on the turf at the tee box. I cried and asked God for something to help me.

The next moment was so real, like the moment Gailya described she had. It was as if I heard David say, "How much do you need, Dad?" Perhaps, and I suspect this was the case, the comment was to be humorous - that was David. He was always that way with me and others he loved and was close to.

Some readers may be beginning to wonder how often I hear words in my head. Perhaps a scoffer would say, "Imagination, and imagination isn't God."

My response: I have learned that in moments of desperation and belief, He will answer when we ask. These moments of words speaking to my heart is God's way. I don't create the comfort; God does. These demonstrations of God's presence go beyond words spoken to my heart.

There, that moment on the fourth tee, I stood to my feet. I looked smiling to the heavens and felt joy.

David is still a comedian. He loves me, and he is aware. Thank you, Lord for allowing the fellowship I still have with my son. I miss the earthly physical touch, but the Lord loves me and is going to get me through.

This morning I glanced over at a plaque I have hanging on the wall that my sister gave me a few years back.

Beginning with that simple glance, a series of experiences began to unfold for me over the next few days, leading up to one of the more supernatural events the Lord has provided me.

The plaque is in the shape of the cross. It has a phrase on it that I had never taken note to be Scripture, because it was taken from a different translation of the Bible than I grew up reading. I recognized it to be a verse of spiritual encouragement, but not exact Scripture.

As long as this plaque had been on the wall, this morning I felt a tug to read it closer. It is titled, "Strength." "Be strong and courageous! Do not be afraid or discouraged.

For the Lord your God is with you wherever you go." - Joshua 1:9

I looked up Joshua 1:9 in the King James Version (KJV) of the Bible, that I had always used, and read it there.

"Have not I commanded thee? Be strong and of a good courage: Be not afraid, neither be thou dismayed: For the Lord thy God is with thee withersoever thou goest." - Joshua 1:9 KJV

Initially I looked at the plaque this morning as I was looking for a place to hang a photo of David I had framed.

The room is designed as the formal living room and is furnished that way; however, I have a roll-top desk in there and use the room as a home office on days I do not go into our corporate office.

I had actually taken the plaque down to see if it fit elsewhere. It was then that I began reading it closer. The spot the plaque was in was a narrow strip between the window and corner, just wide enough for a framed 8 1/2" x 11" photo. You wouldn't notice it being bare. I decided that I really wanted David's picture in that spot, so I set the plaque aside for now, but I also didn't hang David's picture yet.

August 29, 2017

Today would probably be a peak of my worst emotional days.

I had no desire to live any longer.

I haven't referred to this issue yet, but it had been twenty-two days since David had passed, twenty-one days since that morning in his apartment, and every single night since he left, I had checked the clock at some point every hour during the night. For three weeks I had not slept through a sixty minute span. Every night I laid down, my son was on my mind and alive in my heart. Tears flowed most nights, throughout the night. Today I began seriously reflecting that I cannot live this way, unable to escape the sorrow all night, every night.

My blood pressure was out of control, and there seemed to be heart issues developing.
I am somewhat embarrassed to broach this subject, but today taking my life was becoming a constant thought.

I always felt suicide simply could not be an option. I viewed it as the most selfish thing someone could do. I realize there are mental health issues and perhaps even other circumstances that should not be judged under this blanket statement. But generally speaking - again, not judging all - to take your own life is a selfish decision. How could I leave my surviving son whom I love so dearly?

How could I suggest that my love for him was not strong enough to stay here of my choosing and to leave him with such anguish? How could I leave my spouse, who I so love, and ignore her love and need for me? Suicide would be just about my feelings.

Those who know me know I'm programmed to think of others first. I'm thankful for that trait. I am always concerned about how my actions, deeds, or thoughts affect others. How much pain would I bring to my son and my wife if I took my own life?

I'll call it the Devil. He gave me the answer that day. "Marcus, you are going to die. You cannot live without sleep. You are already developing mortal health issues from not sleeping. This is going to kill you. Don't go through all of this pain. You are paining others as well to see you go through this."

The thoughts began to resonate. I became totally comfortable with planning my death. I firmly decided, yes, I would do it; and I began thinking of how to do it. I thought about this the rest of the day and into the evening.

That night, I lay across the foot of our bed, across Iris's legs under the blankets, my head and face slightly covered. Iris was watching TV over me, as the TV is at the foot of the bed. I was wide awake, no sleep in me. I was still thinking about taking my life. Iris had no idea, and I am certain she was not really paying attention to me. My eyes had been open just staring.

I closed my eyes, and immediately, what I can best describe as a vision began.

It was like a full life-sized TV screen, except it wasn't bordered. I was viewing as if my eyes were wide open. The horizon was a royal blue color. I saw from a distance what I knew was my being - me. There was a bridge. I was on the right side of the bridge. On the left side I saw a heavenly being, like an angel, but I knew it was David. I saw this as though from a distance, but then I realized I was there. I was looking across the bridge. David and I were an angelic glowing color. I moved toward the bridge, but David moved toward me, much faster. In an instant, he was in front of me, before I could cross over. He spoke to me.

"It's not your time, Dad. You have to go back."

I immediately threw the covers back and stood up from the bed. The feeling was so daunting! I knew immediately that I was being told that if I tried to kill myself, it would not work. I would have to come back. It was not my time.

Did that mean I would suffer and recover? Would I be paralyzed? I don't know these answers; however, I do know with certainty that God allowed David to visit me in a vision and tell me, "It's not your time, Dad."

I felt God's presence all over me, a warm tingling all over my body, intense and overwhelming!

I don't know if Iris had fallen asleep or if she was deeply engrossed in the TV program.

She didn't seem to notice me. I went down the stairs, shaking!

I realized God had something left for me to do on earth, in this life. I paced constantly back and forth in the living room much of the night - shaking - feeling what I know to be the Lord's presence with me, hearing over and over again, "It's not your time, Dad." I relived the moment over and over again. I wondered: "Did I stop the vision?" It was startling; I had jumped from the bed. "Could I have laid there and let the vision continue?" No, God had done the work He intended.

God moved in my life. He preserved my life for His will to be accomplished in me. He used David. Oh, how blessed I am. Thank you, Lord. Thank you, David.

Sometime the night before, I eventually went back up to bed and slept a couple of hours or so. This morning I was sitting in the living room/office. Iris rarely comes in here as it's more of an at-home office space for me. She tends to be in the family room or the adjoining kitchen area. She is a fantastic chef!

This morning, the morning after the vision, she came in the living room where I was and sat down. Strangely, she asked me, "Didn't you used to have something on the wall here?" She pointed to the area where the plaque had been.

The question was quite odd to me as, again, she doesn't come in here often. I was not at all aware that she noticed what I hung on the walls. I had moved things around in the past on multiple occasions, and I supposed that had gone unnoticed. This area is not an area that begs for wall décor, so I was a little surprised by her asking.

But I explained that I was looking for a place to reposition the plaque and put David's picture in its place.

She held and read the plaque. She then suggested, "Put David's picture on top and the plaque under it."

That was right! It felt perfect. I immediately knew that was the decision to make.

Sitting there, having this conversation, I got a text. About a year and a half before David left us, I contracted a broker agent to join our agency. Gary Hancock was an independent agent, but he desired to be licensed through my agency. Gary began sending me a selected Bible verse every morning. The first time he sent one, I texted back, "Thank you."

When they subsequently came every morning, I thought this was something he did daily, I assumed, to a group of contacts. I did not presume to think it was just to me. Therefore, I did not bother to thank him each day. But I read them each day and was thankful.

This went on for several months. At some point they ceased.

Honestly, I did not take note immediately when they stopped coming. Sometime later, it occurred to me that I no longer received them. That actually made me wonder if perhaps it wasn't a group text and after a time of me not responding perhaps Gary just stopped sending. Whatever the case may be, this is not an agent I talk with often, and when Gary and I did talk, the Scripture texting never came up. It had been now several months since I had received a Bible verse from Gary.

The day before the vision came to me, Gary had just heard about David passing. He called me to offer his condolences, and we chatted some. Nothing was mentioned about the daily Bible Scriptures. Nothing was said about suicidal feelings.

We had a nice conversation and said our goodbyes.

Now, while Iris sat there, Gary had apparently put me back on his daily Bible verse text thread and sent me a new Scripture. I don't think I need to tell anyone how many thousands of Bible verses there are. The one Gary sent me today? Joshua 1:9.

How good is God! How much He loves us! This is not a rare coincidence. This is God's love!

Emotionally, I shared with Iris the last couple of days of events.

It's not easy explaining to your wife you love that you had reached a point of suicide. Telling her about the vision was wonderful. I shared with her the vindication God provided me with the plaque, David's picture placement, and Gary texting me one in thousands of Scriptures, all reminding me God loves us and there is a life left for me to live for God. Indeed, there must be something I need to do. Maybe it is this book, a testimony to strengthen someone else's faith.

I believe Iris saw that God loves us enough to stop suicide. Even when Satan seemed to have control of my emotions, (suicidal thoughts), my soul remained in prayer for God's help, and He answered. God cannot help those that do not look to Him for help. Yes, even while reaching a point of action that would not be pleasing to the Lord, my prayerful spirit brought about God's grace for me. It is to those that believe.

Greater is He that is within me than He that is in the world.

The Lord preserved me this day. As in the past, I called Linda to share with her. I feel compelled to share with her these experiences, believing it will bring her more help and peace as well. These events aren't just for me; that is why I write now. I know David's mom needs God's strength also. David would certainly want me to encourage her.

After we hung up, Linda decided to look up the Scripture (Joshua 1:9) in the Bible she had given David for Christmas some previous year. She called me back to tell me about it. As she flipped the pages of David's Bible, she stumbled onto where David had marked with pen some Scriptures.

He marked Lamentations 3:25, 26, 32.

25   "The Lord is good unto them that wait for him, to the soul that seeketh him."

26   "It is good that a man should hope and quietly wait for the salvation of the Lord."

32   "But though he causes grief, yet will he have compassion according to the multitude of his mercies."

Not only did the Scripture he marked prove further to me that David's heart was right with God and that David lived by God's grace, the actual text of the Scriptures showed me His position with God - saved!

My son did honor God, praise God, desire more of God!

The last couple of days has been the salvation of my soul. The Lord is good, the Lord is great! He is my peace. I may continue to miss David in the days ahead, and grief may still grip me some, but I rest assured God saved my son. He has proven Himself to me to be the only omnipotent God. His grace and love are beyond human comprehension.

God is wonderful! The last 24 hours since the vision: Peaceful. I understand more. I ask God to thank David. I can feel his presence with me, so strong!

The Lord has been doing a work in my life. I had gone from total desperation to knowing that my son is safe, happy, and at peace with the Lord. I know it. God has wonderfully moved to provide that confidence, and maybe I'm on the road to more understanding that God's foreknowledge of our lives destines us to a life of purpose. David's life in that dimension with the Lord has a purpose.

Still, how human and frail I am. God has moved supernaturally to provide me strength, yet in the days, weeks and months ahead, and I am sure years to come, until I go home, there will be days of human sorrow. There will be days of temptation to ask, "Why?" When that occurs, I look to the Lord. He is merciful to again and again provide me what I need.

Iris and I were having dinner at our kitchen counter this day.

We were mostly done. She took our dog Duncan outside.

I sat there alone staring at the dinner dishes and began thinking about "near death experiences" (NDEs). I recalled reading about some. I also recalled the time someone I knew shared an experience they had of dying. Brother William Branham told the story of his wife passing. Fervently he prayed at her bedside, "God bring her back!"

Brother Branham was a devout believer of the Lord's power to heal the sick and raise the dead.

He had experienced God's grace in these areas throughout his ministry, with many miracles. The Lord had revealed to him that if you can just get the people to believe, all things are possible. This day his prayer and belief were for his wife. He tells how when he prayed, she opened her eyes and immediately asked him, "Why did you bring me back, Bill? I was almost there - Heaven - beautiful!"

A physical therapist I went to in the past had shared with me her personal experience. She died, and the doctors were trying to revive her. She told me suddenly she was in such a beautiful place and did not want to come back.

I read a book, Proof of Heaven, written by a neurosurgeon, recounting his own personal experience. He was clinically dead, and it was scientifically impossible for him to come back. When he did come back, he wrote of all of his experiences and the beauty of Heaven, with the recurring theme: he didn't want to come back.

I have greatly shortened the stories, but the emphasis for me is that these people all had passed on and all had one similar thought/ feeling/desire: they did not want to come back.

Suddenly, alone at the kitchen counter in our home,

I found myself having a seemingly live conversation with David. I felt David, and I spoke audibly. This was not a vision. I was sitting in my chair and softly spoke, "David, you would come back for a while, wouldn't you?"

I'm sure I was thinking, "You love us; you would come back for a little while, wouldn't you?"

"Are you crazy?" I could hear his voice so plainly say, as though someone was whispering in my ear, though not audibly. My son used that phrase so often when he was with us. I cannot illustrate in written words the voice inflection he used. Just a comical, sarcastic but respectful, "Are you crazy?"

Then, with sincerity:

"You can come here someday." "Serve the Lord."

Those words rang in my ears, and I could sense his exact tone.

It was, indeed, as if I were having a conversation with David.

This wasn't a vision; this wasn't an illusion. I also refute any attempt to say it's my creative mind and my hunger for my son's relationship. This was God allowing David to speak to my heart. I know this with all conviction; I felt his presence.

To those who read this, believe God. Pray, believing, for the needs you have. He will answer in His time. His time is the right time.

The last line I felt in my heart from David was equally important to me: "Serve the Lord."

I firmly believe these writings are a part of that mission God has for my life, to share His grace

He has provided to me. It's for you, as well, if you but ask and believe.

Also the same for you: "Serve the Lord."

It was some time before I sat and viewed the video of my son's memorial service. Obviously, I have not mentioned that day. This book is about life, promise, healing of the spirit, God's love and David's home that I will make my own someday.

I will briefly recap the service. I didn't make it through it.

During the service I began to sweat and became very pale. My brother-in-law stepped up and gave me a bottle of water. I passed out and slumped to the floor.

I awoke, just moments later, lying in the middle aisle on my back, surrounded by those close to me. I remember the minister instructing the congregation to pray for me and questioning whether to continue or not. I strained to lift my head from the floor and looked directly into his eyes, saying, "Please continue." The service was concluded. I was transported to the hospital. The interment was delayed a few days.

I have no memory of the minister's sermon. So today, September 17th, I sat and viewed the service. I desired to hear the words of the minister, Brother Joe Greene. He spoke of King David losing his son. He quoted King David saying, "I can't bring him back, but I can go to him."

The same words that God had spoken to my heart and said to me in the shower that day I described earlier!

Doubters of what I testify to may try to say that I heard Brother Joe Greene talk on this Scriptural incident in King David's life during my son's memorial service. However, the Lord being my witness, I did not hear him or recall it. Scoffers may say my sub-conscience heard it. My sub-conscience didn't speak to me in the shower that morning; the God of Heaven did!

Just as God had provided those words to King David during his troubled time, the same Lord delivered this message to me that morning in the shower, days later during my turmoil. "You can't bring him back, but you can go to him someday."

The Lord ordained the sermon by Brother Greene, and used it to confirm His promise in my life. This is God directly working in my life and providing me deliverance and peace: David is safe in Heaven! Supernatural event? God working miracles of peace in my life because I pray, believe, and look to Him for direction? You better believe it!

Shortly after this, my son Daniel called me. Needless to say, the strains on my heart to have led David in the ways of the Lord weigh on me equally for the son I am blessed to have with me today. Daniel is two years older than David. They grew up very close and remained such through their young adulthood. When Daniel called me, he told me that a page in his Bible was creased unknowingly.

When he opened his Bible today, it fell open to some of King David's writings. My, the Lord is so mindful of us and those we love. The Lord using King David's writings to provide assurance for my son Daniel!

Daniel had some spiritual and Biblical questions for me today. He told me during this conversation that he has become more aware of the life that he lives and has a growing desire to do right in the sight of God. Daniel went on to ask me some questions about certain things in life and what the Bible taught regarding them.

Today, Daniel reaching for me, Dad, for spiritual guidance was a tremendous gift from God! I'll live my entire life to influence my son to put God first and teach him that God will direct his paths. Having lived so long with doubts that I had provided enough spiritual guidance for my sons was such a burden on my soul. God is not only restoring and preserving me, His love is granting me my deepest heart's desire, the salvation of my sons and of my wife. I know God has given me all I love and is faithful to provide for us now and into eternity together.

The Lord did not take my son David purposefully to strengthen me nor to draw Daniel closer to him. But He did promise to bring about good in our lives when we lean on Him during these painful times.
"All things work together for good, to them that love the Lord."

Losing David's direct fellowship in this life... well, the Lord is certainly doing a work in all of our lives during this time. Life's troubles aren't to make us strong. But during these times God will reach down and draw us closer to Him if we only rely on Him with all of our hearts.

All of God's grace and strength given me, yet the frailty and humanity never cease to creep in. Sorrow. Missing David's fellowship grieves my heart.

The Lord constantly proves to me that He is ever mindful of the state we find ourselves in. He is ever mindful, and without ceasing He provides little nuggets of strength. The next moment was one of those times.

I am usually quite organized. However, sometimes things that I mean to organize, and file aren't filed in a fashion that I know where to look or even remember I have them. Today I came across something my sister Phyllis passed on to me after Naomi went to be with the Lord. Naomi wrote it and laminated it but never mentioned it to me, and Phyllis found it in her personal things not long after she passed. I read it at the time and filed it away.

Today I came across it, and today it was meant by God for me to find, as it would again provide strength that only the Lord can give us.

My sister had a dream on November 3, 1994. She wrote, "Marcus was working on a job but did not receive the income he expected. When he left the job, he came back crippled, walking with a cane. He thought he was well, but all of a sudden, he wasn't. Climbing up a hill with a cane, he fell on his back and sank in the sand deep enough for a body print, about halfway.

I [Naomi] got over his body and a 'message came.' As I began to speak the message, Marcus was saying, 'I thought I was well.'

I [Naomi] thought he was going to continue to out-talk me while the message was coming forth, but the message continued to come, and he stopped and listened."

The message was, "If you will commit your ways to me, I will heal you and make you whole."

Finding this today, with its message saved for me by my sister, is God again restoring my spirit, providing His love and comfort.

I cannot express how uplifting, how inspirational, and how awesome God's timing is, to provide these nuggets in our time of emotional need. No matter how many times my strength slips, my joy dwindles, God is a provider to them that diligently seek Him. Every day I realize how much I need the Lord as Master of my life.

As I worked in my yard, thoughts of David being gone from me grieved me so. I cried, as I do every day. As I ponder all the experiences God has given me to help me get through, to let me know constantly that He is with me, that He is in control, that He loves me, the assurances that David is okay...I still fail. Even with all of the experiences, the spiritual divine touches, the miraculous inspirations provided to keep me going, I still fall back into sorrow.

This day I prayed aloud, "Lord, help me be strong. How can I help others if I keep falling?"

While I prayed, I had the feeling I must be strong. I immediately asked in my heart, as if I was having a conversation with God, "Why do I have to be the strong one?"

The answer came immediately. "Because the promise is greater...remain faithful over a few things, I'll make you ruler over many." God's Scriptural words.

I immediately remembered Naomi's dream. I prayed aloud and asked God for the healing of my spirit and my pain. Those were my exact words.

One hour later, Brother Louie texted me to say, "Listen to this." He asked me to look up this song entitled, "Healing is Here."

My, my, the Lord is again so mindful and hears our needs and is readily there to meet them.

There is nothing coincidental about this event. God is so on point with us and specific. "Marcus, healing is here. I not only will heal your sickness; I will heal your spirit and soul."

When these experiences began occurring in my life, I had no thought of writing a book. I thank God that I did realize the wisdom of putting the events down on paper. This was done for my own memory, to be able to go back and read when my spirit needed a jolt in low times and depression. This would remind me of how great and real God has made Himself in my life. I now realize these writings may help someone, hopefully many, to reach out to God and allow Him to be real in their lives. I am no more special than anyone else. He is there if we ask. I am reminded in the Scriptures it states, "Ye ask, and receive not, because you ask amiss…"

This is God in my life. We all have a purpose here. The journey to Heaven has some very rough roads, but God's strength is there for us.

Linda, Daniel, and Iris belong to God. I know they have experienced the Lord's strength through this time in our lives.

I don't know how prevalent or frequently they have experiences like mine. However, when they have shared theirs with me, I made little notes of these as well. I do not know every circumstance that may have occurred in their lives preceding the event, nor subsequent surrounding circumstances after the event.

I interject them in my writings, as I know they are also a part of God helping me. It's helping me because God is saying, "Marcus, I love Daniel; I love Iris; I love Linda. You are all mine. Live for me. Live the testimony."

The following is one simple event shared with me:
Not dated
Linda told me:

"Marcus, it was a very personal moment. I was in the shower. I asked God to forgive me for something." She told me that it was so real, as if she heard it audibly.

"I forgive you, and David is here" (meaning in God's presence - with the Lord).

Some will read this as so simple. I read it and write it as a message from God.

David was at a family outing the day before he went home to be with the Lord. The outing was at one of his aunt's home. His Aunt Vickie told us how kind, sweet, and personable he was that day. He reached out and hugged her and said so sincerely, "Vickie, how are you?" Vickie told us it was so sweet the way David had done that.

There was such a peace about David that day.

The next day, Monday, August 7, 2017, was David's last day in the office. I was told later how peaceful, calm, and considerate David was that day at work.

That evening, his mom stopped by his home. She saw David in the parking lot. Linda said the brief conversation they had together as she sat in her car showed such a sweet spirit about David.

God had done the work in my son's heart! He was ready to meet the Lord. That evening, he did.

My tears flow like a river now, but with peace and longing for our reunion.

Texting Linda, "Pray for you - you for me." I sent her the song Brother Louie sent me, "Healing is Here." Calling her, I shared the significance of the story behind it. When I got to the part about me praying for the healing of my spirit, she said in her own words exactly what Brother Louie had said to me when he sent me the song. "Christ has always been with you. He never will leave you." She continued, "He is that perfect love."

I had the song playing low in the background as I was talking with Linda. It is very doubtful she could hear it. As she stated those words to me, "He is that perfect love," I realized that exact line of the song was being played simultaneously as Linda was speaking those words!

Coincidence? I say no, God loves us that much. He constantly reveals Himself to us and shows He cares that we live in communication with Him. It is God's perfect plan to reveal Himself and His love to me and to us all; and also for me - that David is safe in God's presence waiting for reunion day!

A close friend, Alyson, called me later this day just to say, "God is with you. David is with God. David is in His majesty."

I'm reminded of the song, "The Love of God."

"The love of God is greater far than tongue or pen can ever tell.
It goes beyond the highest star and reaches to the lowest hell." Another excerpt:
"Could we with ink the ocean fill and were the skies of parchment made,
Were every stalk on earth a quill and every man a scribe by trade, To write the love of God above would drain the ocean dry,
Nor could the scroll contain the whole, though stretched from sky to sky."

Frederick M. Lehman, 1917

Becca, an agent in my organization, had only been with us a short while when David left. She barely knew him, but she was inspired, I believe by God, to write a poem for me, for David. I share it with you now.

I'm Free

"Don't grieve for me, for now I'm free.
I'm following the path God has laid for me. I took His hand when I heard Him call.
I turned my back and left it all. I could not stay another day To laugh, to love, to work, to play. Tasks left undone must stay that way. I found that peace at the close of day. If my parting has left a void,
Then fill it with remembered joy:
A friendship shared, a laugh, a kiss - Oh yes, those things I will miss.
Be not burdened with tones of sorrow. I wish you the sunshine of tomorrow. My life's been full; I've savored much- Good friends, good times, a loved one's touch. Perhaps my time seemed all too brief.
Don't lengthen it now with undue grief. Lift up your hearts, and peace to thee! God wanted me now. He set me free."

- My Friend, Becca Sharits

October 14, 2017

No matter how real God reveals Himself to me, shows His love to me, provides me full assurance that David is in that Heavenly dimension waiting gloriously for the day of our reunion, sorrow and pain returns. When we're being of service for the Lord and totally happy and at peace, it is obviously Satan's full-time mission to buffet us, taunt us, try us, tempt us and cause us pain.

Notice I didn't say doubt God's promises. I will never doubt God. Still, today, but for a few moments, the pain and sorrow overwhelm me. I ashamedly say, that suicide spirit the Lord delivered me from, again presented itself to me. Immediately, God's presence was on the scene for me. It might have felt a little chastising, lecturing.

In these moments of grief and sorrow, we don't always know, nor even think about at the moment, how to get out of that stupor. That's why I say, "God came on the scene." I have learned that if we commit our ways to Him, He is faithful in all of our needs.

Immediately thoughts from God occurred to me. Daniel wondering about my love for him, the pain it would cause him, to carry that burden the rest of his life, Dad leaving this life that way.

The pain it would cause Iris my wife. Linda no doubt would grieve for Daniel as well as for herself.

David would surely be upset with me for not staying there for his brother, his mom, his stepmom. David would surely be grieved with me.

The vision said, "It's not my time." I cannot disobey. All would be lost. My soul, being with my children again, and eternity.

Satan is such a liar and a deceiver. I enter heaven through the blood of Jesus Christ and faithfulness. Remember, David told me, "Serve the Lord."

These thoughts came to me as real as a sermon or lecture as soon as that tempter approached me.

All of us, serve the Lord, He will never forsake us in our hour of need.

The past week had difficult times. I prayed; I sought God; I waited on Him. This morning I found myself emotionally summarizing the challenges of the past week.

As I sat reflecting, I reached for today's mail. There was a sympathy card from one of my clients, Christine Lyon. The card referred to the writings in the Bible: "To everything there is a season." She further stated, "May faith, hope, and love give you the strength you need." The words were all so good for me to read this day, so needed.

I sat there realizing how much the Lord was watching over me, not because I'm special, but because I have asked believing, knowing that God will deliver and answer. He answers before we even ask sometimes. He knows our hearts. This was happening for me right now. I could plainly feel God's presence with me as I read the card. The Lord is aware, He is watching, and He loves me.

I turned the envelope over, and there was God's confirmation for me. The return address was a small town in North Carolina, and the street name was "Saint David Street."

Brother Louie texted me today. He gave me the words, "Be bold, be strong, for the Lord thy God is with thee." It resounded in my soul. I responded, "How difficult some days are, but I believe what you said - God is with me. I believe it more than ever in my lifetime."

Brother Louie texted back, "When God starts a work in our lives, nothing can stop it." That was so encouraging to me. God is in control. He has started a work in my life, and He will complete it. Such comfort. Thank you, Lord!

For Daniel's birthday, which is October 29th, the family decided to go see a movie, "Let There Be Light."

We discussed the emotional difficulty in going to see it. It is based on a true story of a father that lost his young son. This guy was a staunch atheist. He taunted believers and wrote a book slamming Christians. His spouse and children were Christians.

The reviews of the movie indicated the father would be in a tragic auto accident and indeed die in the ambulance. Subsequently, he would have a near death experience, NDE.

We all knew the movie could be painful, but I was compelled to go see it. This was a 'low-cost' production movie and would only have limited run times in our area. The drawing in my soul to go see the movie, I know now, was the Lord. I am finding the Lord anxious to bless and strengthen us as believers.

With all of that said, I still presented the idea to the family of going only if it were a unanimous decision, and it was. Linda, Daniel and Iris all said, "Let's go." Daniel's fiancé, Jennifer, joined us as well. (They are to be married next year. God has tremendously blessed Daniel and our family with Jennifer.)

As stated earlier, we were all getting together for Daniel's birthday.

This day was the only movie run time we would all be able to view it together. We were going out to dinner for Daniel's birthday celebration afterward.

The beginning of the movie depicted the father's lifestyle, his atheistic viewpoints, and his belittling of Christians. Prior to his auto accident in the movie, he was celebrating the release of his new book that slams Christianity. The celebration was at a party where he drank alcohol to excess. Upon leaving the party, he chose to drive and subsequently was in a violent crash. This was maybe 15 minutes into the movie.

In the ambulance, being transferred to the hospital, all of his vital signs ceased. Immediately the movie showed him walking toward a very bright light. Moments later, his young departed son appeared, walking out of the light toward his father. Standing astonished and in amazement, his son reached him. The first words from his son's mouth were, "It's not your time, Dad, you have to go back."

Immediately my entire body began to shiver - God's presence around me. I immediately turned and looked at Daniel, Linda, Iris, and Jenn. They all knew the words I heard David speak to me in my vision - exact words! I stood up in that theater without hesitation, with great respect and acknowledgement of God visiting us with His promise. A confirmation again of the vision He had given me on that suicidal feeling night.

I stood and honored my Lord, as I know I felt His presence with us in that theater. It was not by chance that I had come across this little-publicized production. I'm not saying the Lord of Heaven had it produced and filmed just for us, but I will testify until eternity that it was made for us, as well as for whomever else God planned. Many months before this time in our lives - losing David in this earthly life - God knew what we would go through. He knew our needs long before they occurred. Yes, I know He allowed this movie to be prepared and provided at the exact time we would need it. He loves us that much! I am sure it was prepared for many others that needed it as well. I was one of them.

No coincidence; God is too "spot on." The formula is exact. We serve a perfect God!

Today is my first birthday without David. I am remembering how he and Daniel always came to see me on my birthday. David always reached out and hugged me when he arrived and said, "Happy birthday." He always gave me a goofy birthday card. He is the one that always chose a comical type of card. It was always the humorous perspective of a father's and son's relationship. This day was difficult, an emotional day for me. I texted Brother Louie, fearful of getting through the long day. I was fearful that I would be so broken up; and with family and friends expected to come over in the evening, well, I just didn't want to be that way when they all arrived. I don't like putting that emotional burden on those around me. I love and appreciate the support they give; however, I hate putting that sadness on them. I know how it is to wish you could help someone through their sorrows, yet feel so helpless for them. I could not see this day being a good day. I so much wanted to see Daniel, my wife, my friends, but then I would hate myself for burdening them so.

I have so well learned, God cares and loves us, and has it all worked out, even before we pray. The Lord saw my trepidation and sorrow. The miracle of a blessing was already sanctioned, and I didn't know what God was about to do for me.

Brother Louie texted me back, "Be bold, be strong, for the Lord thy God is with thee."

I prayed for inner strength.

I felt in my soul God starting to intervene in my day.

I had been putting off a to-do task of cleaning out a file drawer. Many times, I had put it on my to-do list but would just mark it off and not get it done by the end of that day. It had actually been months since I first put it on my to-do list. I simply just kept putting it off.

After Brother Louie's text, I told Iris I would be going through some files on the third floor, should she wonder where I was. Being an organized type of guy, I didn't like a file becoming a junk drawer, and today was the day to tackle it. This file drawer had personal business items: old mortgage files, expired warranties, obsolete owner manuals, etc. - items that needed purging, but no mementos and personal papers of a private nature. Not even a couple minutes into the sorting, I found a printed copy of an email my mom had sent me on my birthday, December 10, 2002. Fifteen years later - to the day - I found this email in a file it should not have been in!

Today, I came across this misfiled letter from my mom, sent to me on my birthday fifteen years before. Of all the days that I had planned to clean out these files, today I got to it.

Marcus, do you think God put that in there? Well, I know He can do anything. He created the heavens and earth. This is a small thing.

Did He direct me to misfile it years before, awaiting the day I would need it more? God's foreknowledge, I guarantee you so!

The letter from my mom contained some Scripture for me: Psalm 118:24 - "This is the day the Lord has made, let us rejoice and be glad in it."

You think God knew I would need that Scripture today? You bet He did!

Numbers 6:24-26 - "The Lord bless you and keep you; the Lord make His face shine upon you, and be gracious to you; the Lord lift up His countenance upon you and give you peace."

You think God loved me today and knew fifteen years ago how much I would need His grace today? I know He did!

Philippians 1:3 - "I thank my God every time I remember you." Mom's love also...thank you, Lord, for that.

Psalm 128:5 - "May the Lord bless you from Zion all the days of your life."

God's love.

How much more directly can God and does God speak to us when we need him?

We often hear scoffers make light of someone saying, "God spoke to me." God speaks to His children in many ways. He speaks when we need it. He speaks when we cry out to Him and believe.

The Lord this day has spoken directly to me and as real as the day He spoke to Moses from the burning bush.

I am frail; I am weak. No doubt I will need Him again, but God is there for us! His promises are real! On our saddest days, remember He is with us. He will deliver, and we will smile and feel His joy right in the midst of the storm.

Thank you, Lord. May every child of yours that reads this be blessed and feel your touch right at the moment they read this, as you have done for me. Amen!

I have an attorney, Tyler, whose paralegal is Lorie. They both knew David well. I stopped in on this day to chat with Tyler, but he wasn't in, and Lorie asked me to sit down in her office.

It had only been five months since David had left to be in the Lord's presence. This was the first time Lorie and I had spoken since David left, and he would be our entire conversation.

I felt compelled to share with Lorie God's gifts to me by way of these experiences. I always feel God's presence so close when I share them.

Lorie then told me about an event surrounding the passing of her mom. She was with her mom and was aware the moment was near. She made a request of her mom: send her two white doves when she was in Heaven.

Lorie was quite detailed in describing the first few days afterwards her mother passed. Some days later, a good friend of hers asked for help moving.

Lorie described the event: sorting, packing, loading boxes, etc.

Some items were being left intentionally. However, as they were about to back out of the driveway, Lorie's friend remembered an item she needed. Lorie went back in to retrieve it.

There were other boxes on the porch, some of the things left intentionally. As she was picking up the thing she came for, Lorie heard something scratching inside one of the boxes. She set the item down and went across the porch to the box the noise came from. She slowly reached down and opened the box.

Two white doves!

Her friend had totally forgotten she had left them. Lorie had no idea her friend owned such a thing!

Lorie and I had a very inspiring conversation and counted it another blessing from God to strengthen me and once again affirm God's love for us and His ever mindfulness of our needs.

I came home after leaving my attorney's office and visit with Lorie. As I reflected on Lorie's story, even though God has already given me so much in the way of assurances of David's place in Heaven, I still once again asked God to let me know that David is aware of the things we do for his memory and that he knows I love him so much!

I didn't ask for a specific fleece as did Lorie; I just prayed this request of the Lord.

The next morning, less than twenty-four hours later, Wayne, an agent of mine and dear brother in the Lord called me. Wayne's first words to me were that He felt led of God to call me and tell me that there is a Scripture in the Bible ("I don't know where it is," he stated) that a minister once told him of.

"The saints in heaven are aware of us and are cheering us on!"

Less than a day earlier, I asked God to reveal to me that David is aware of our love and the memories we have. God directly leads a brother to answer that prayer. Not a coincidence: this is our heavenly Father loving us, caring for us, and directly answering prayer. Once again God assured me David is in Heaven. Thank you, Lord!

The following is very simple, and I realize some will say, "Marcus, that is just positive mental attitude." I am very much a believer of what positive thinking can do for all of us, but I have learned the difference between it and the presence of God working in my life.
The verse Wayne had referenced was:

"Wherefore seeing we also are compassed about with so great a cloud of witnesses...." Hebrews 12:1

I know David is aware of me, as well as of his brother, mother, step-mom, etc. I know God allows him to assist us on some level. This afternoon I was out on the golf course, practicing on the putting green. This part of my game by far needs the most work. I am just not a good reader of the greens and not at all consistent with my putting stroke.

I was practicing a twelve-foot putt. On my best day, I may sink one out of ten. In standing over my next putt, David was on my mind, and I asked God for assurance that he is close. In an instant I felt David speak to me and say, "Commit to it." I knew what he meant: Execute what I know to do. Commit to the putt. I did, with total confidence. I sank the next three twelve-foot putts. I can tell you I have never done that!

The most important lesson I learned wasn't golf related. It was that David is near and mindful of us. Also,

God answers prayer.

I said this event was simple, and some would say not everything that happens to you is God related. I adamantly disagree. If I live in God's presence and ask believing, He will always be there for me as well as for anyone reading this. Might I also add, God has given me, over the first six months since David left us, one hundred percent assurance that David is in that realm the Lord has prepared for us.

Daniel called me this morning. He opened up some with me, more so than in the past. He carries much within himself silently. He told me that he mourns daily that he didn't tell David enough, "I love you." He told me that he often wishes that he could hug him.

This particular morning, he had an experience with David, and it compelled him to call me. The experience involved Facebook. He had just been thinking that he wished he could hug David. I have no familiarity with Facebook. Daniel attempted to explain a feature to me. Apparently, Facebook today notified Daniel he has a shared memory and had been tagged. I understand from Daniel that's an automatic feature Facebook uses to notify one that a year ago (anniversary), this person sent you this.

Daniel opened the "tag." It was a picture David had sent him a year before of them hugging! The photo was one taken three years before that. After long searches, Daniel found where David had originally sent it to him. Either Daniel had never received it back when David originally sent it, or Daniel somehow overlooked it back a year ago.

Daniel said he hates that he never saw it when David originally sent it; however, how great is God! The grace of God, the love of God- for that "tag" to be chosen and sent while Daniel was so grieving. It wasn't meant to be seen a year ago. God had a greater purpose. God knew that Daniel would need it now.

The evil one, Satan, attempted to turn it around to plague Daniel with the thought of not having responded to David a year before, adding to Daniel's burden of mourning, as he wishes he had told David more often that he loved him.

I told Daniel that is Satan, the evil spirit in this world, that tries to deny you God's gifts. The gift God sent you today is that David is aware of you; he loves you, and he knows you love him. He sent you that hug today. Facebook doesn't "tag" everything.

God allowed David to do that for Daniel, just as I have witnessed in my life.

"The love of God, how rich and pure, how measureless and strong."

I stood on the golf practice range at Hasentree today. I came to attempt a practice session. Practicing is something I have always enjoyed since the day I first picked up the game, later in life than most.

It has been eight months since David left us. He was my golf buddy and the one I played more rounds with. Probably seventy-five percent of the time I played; it was with my son. Those times will stay with me forever.

Up until this day, I have often wondered if I will ever get the joy back in playing. I know in my soul David would want me to play and enjoy the relaxation and cherish our memories.

With all of that said, today will prove to be one of the most miraculous days the Lord has provided me of consolation, of knowledge that David is aware and near me often, and, indeed, watching over me.

Today is practice. I took a spot on the range and did some normal warmups and stretching. David was not in the forefront of my mind at this moment. Seemingly there is hardly a day, a moment that he is but an eye blink away from my thoughts. However, at this particular time I wasn't dwelling in that space. My thoughts were focused on practicing.

Rarely am I totally alone on the range. Usually someone or, most of the time, a few others are out doing the same as I. Today the range was deserted. It was just me. Practice, when I am actively hitting balls, is not a procedure of just repeatedly dropping balls and hitting them one after another. I am disciplined to work on particular shots, and my routine is slow and deliberate. I place the ball, mentally plan my shot, take my alignment and stance, address the ball with the club- face, and after a moment make my swing and strike the ball. Today was no different. Place the ball, check my alignment, check my stance and ball position, position the club addressing the ball, check my target, two or three seconds, make my swing.

I do not recall, at the time I am writing this down, how many practice shots I had made. It was very early in my session. It could not have been but a couple shots or so when the Lord stepped in with a mighty blessing.

As always, on this next practice shot, I had placed the ball, I had the club head placed directly behind the ball grounded, I glanced at my target, and then my pause before taking my backswing. A millisecond before I would take my backswing, in the distance a crow made that loud "caw" sound they make. But it was distinctly different. It was ever so clear. Unmistakably, the sound of "maaaa-cus." It wasn't a one syllable sound.

It was distinctive, double-syllabled and the sound of my name in that "caw" monotone.

David had often called me by my name pronounced that way, that same exact sound. It was always on the golf course and in a moment of jest with me. I may say something or make some comment, maybe even about a golf shot. He would say, "Oh Maaa-cus." Then he would laugh. It was an expression he had with me, as if to say, "Are you kidding me?"

I struggle to put in print the clarity of what I heard.

As soon as I heard the crow mimic exactly the name and sound David had often done with me, I froze in place standing over my ball, my head still down, frozen there for a moment. Was this a surreal moment? No, I knew immediately in my heart it was God providing me an incredible moment, a time of assurance, solidifying my faith. With that said, I knew it was a crow. I know their sound is so similar. But I know I heard my name in the same double-syllable, monotone of David. Still I just stood there for a moment refusing to look up that way. The sound came from my right side. After what felt like a minute wait, I looked up at my target and took my shot.

I took a few extra seconds watching the flight of my ball. As I thought about what just happened, I knew ninety-nine out of one hundred people would just say I was delusional.

I did not want to deny what I immediately felt was God working with me in a supernatural way, but I realized the skepticism that would no doubt be voiced if I related this event.

I slowly stepped back, looking downrange, and began constructing my next practice shot. I deliberately did not look over in the direction I had heard the sound. I went through the same methodical succession of placing the ball for my next shot and getting positioned over the ball to make another shot.

I was so deliberate and disciplined in moving on with another shot that, the Lord as my witness, somehow I put what had just happened out of my mind. I resumed my focus on hitting the next practice shot. After all, wasn't it probably just a regular crow sound?

The event repeated. After placing the ball for my shot, assuming my stance, a look at my target, and about to take my backswing, the same identical moment, the crow did it again. It was so plain and louder... so clearly double-syllable: "Maaa-cus!" In that "caw" sound.

This time I immediately looked up, straight to the direction I heard the sound. The building they store golf carts in for the course is a simple "A" frame roof, approximately seventy-five yards away; there on the apex of the roof stood a large black crow. As soon as I saw him, my eyes went directly to his eyes. Seventy-five yards away, but we were eye to eye, and I could see his eyes so clearly. It was a very brief moment, for as soon as I looked up and caught its eye, it flew off. I could not have startled that creature from that distance with a simple look. As soon as I acknowledged its visit, it flew off.

I trust you reading this by now have correctly assumed that I am not a believer in reincarnation; my son is not a crow. My son is a son of God. He is not dwelling in a crow. God can and does use vessels to speak to us sometimes. I know He allowed David to do the same.

I am reminded throughout the Scriptures of God doing this.

He spoke to Moses from a burning bush. God used a donkey to speak to Balaam in the book of Numbers. He led Israel by fire at night and a cloud by day. The Lord can certainly allow David to speak to me through a crow, and He did this day. My son David always called me Dad, but in fun moments, on multiple occasions, on the golf course, David would say, "Oh Maaaaa-cus!"

David sent me a message this day: "Enjoy golf, Dad. You have our memories." The Lord let me know this day that David is aware of my well-being. He loves me and will see me again in glory. But for now, "Enjoy, Dad...Maaaaa-cus!"

God gave me this moment alone on the range, even though I had not asked. He visited me in my time of need and allowed David to do the same.

Thank you, Lord! Thank you, David! I love you, son!

This is one of those days that, even as sorrow tempted me, I am reminded of all the special visitations the Lord has given me. Each and every time my needs reached desperation; God came on the scene for me.
How deep God's love is for us, if we but lean on Him daily. Live a believer's life; God will never fail us.

This day, as I'm just reflecting on this, I remember the Scripture, "Confess your faults one to another, and pray for one another, that ye may be healed. The effectual fervent prayer of a righteous man availeth much." As I went about in faith in God this day, the Lord brought that Scripture to memory. I researched the verse and found it in God's Word in James 5:16.

I am not a Bible scholar. I have never endeavored to memorize Scriptures, and I do not have a photographic memory, as a few people do. I do have God with me daily, the One that is able to bring all things to our memory. (I believe that is a Scriptural statement as well.)

In case you are wondering how this fit into my book on God's given experiences He has blessed me with to assure me of David's safety in Heaven and the eternal home I shall someday live in with my loved ones, it's quite simple. All can choose, by your free will to live daily, prayerfully, to please God in all of your life. He will always be there.

The Lord providing me this Scriptural memory today, without searching, validates even more every experience He has given me.

In rapid succession, after the Lord reminding me of this Scripture in James, almost without pause my memory again recalled a Scripture that said, "He gives us the desires of our hearts." I searched the Bible and found, "Delight thyself also in the Lord and He will give thee the desires of thine heart." Psalm 37:4

The Lord is so real and available for us in our daily lives if we but rely on Him and be faithful.

The Lord has given me some supernatural experiences, and this simple day is no less supernatural for me. He is proving to me how peaceful and rewarding life will be if we live in His presence.

Struggle with issues the world throws at us daily, if you want. If you truly give it to Him, no matter what it is — job, finances, love, world events, sickness, heartache, — He will direct you and give you peace. He knows every one of us; He is aware. Release your pride. Forget what others may think. God is real, and He has all of our answers, if we but ask and believe.

My friend Alyson called me late one night. She wanted to share an experience that had just happened to her, but was a bit hesitant, unsure how I would respond.

I realize that there will be skeptics who will reason away everything I have said, disbelieving that our Lord is indeed our loving God and is more than willing to provide all we need. Alyson had similar concerns with me before calling. She wasn't sure how I would receive it. Little did she know how much God had been working with me and been there for me through this time in my life.

Alyson told me that she had drifted off to sleep. She suddenly awoke and her room seemed filled with smoke. She heard something and knew it was David. After a moment she heard him speak. "Tell Dad to remember the time he hugged me and told me he was proud of me. Tell him I am proud of him."

A couple of months before David left us, we were chatting in my, office about how he was doing at work and personally.

In our conversation, quizzing him as a dad would do, I discovered a financial burden he had. After thorough discussion, I chose to relieve that burden for him; I wrote the checks. I explained the reason I was doing so.

I felt because of the level of anxiety David was experiencing, it would be a good thing for him physically and emotionally for me to do this. As thankful as he was, he reminded me, "Dad, you don't have to do this."

This was a good moment with my son. I embraced him in a hug.

As I did so, I told him, "I am so proud of you, Son."

While there are many times in our lives we hug our children, and indeed assure them of how proud we are of them, this particular time, two months before David must leave us was a specific and particularly special moment.

When Alyson related her experience to me, I knew her visitation was real, and God allowed David to communicate to me through Alyson's experience. Not only was I reminded of my time with David that day, but in his speech to Alyson, it was David's, "Tell Dad" that made it real.

"Tell Dad to remember the time he hugged me and told me he was proud of me. Tell Him I am proud of him."

I know David is very proud that this sorrow of losing his earthly fellowship has turned me closer to God.

There was the time where I felt David speak to me and say, "Serve the Lord, Dad." This came back to me as Alyson replayed her experience to me.

So much was in this visitation. Being reassured that David is aware of our lives, his safety with the Lord, the specificity of this experience.

While losing your child's fellowship in this life has got to be one of the most difficult times one can have in their lifetime, the joy the Lord has available for us to get through trumps the trials. I will always miss David until I am with him in glory, but the Lord so graciously has provided me a relationship I never thought possible. A relationship with God and my son David. The Lord will do this for anyone that believes and puts their daily faith in Him.

That meeting I had with David was a closed-door meeting, one I had never shared with anyone. My life has grown closer to God and my son David is proud of that in me. How good is that?!

I later shared this experience with Linda. She told me that the day I paid off David's credit cards, he told her about it and was so excited and happy! She said he almost shouted it: "Mom, Dad paid off my credit cards!" This day, David sent me his message, "Dad, I am so proud of you! Serve the Lord."

It has been nine months since David went home to that dimension our Lord provides of peace and love. I know this to be true more so than ever before in my life.

Today the autopsy report came in the mail. It's a day I needed to face, things I needed to know at some point, yet dreaded - so tremendously dreaded - to read. I knew in my heart the natural issue that took David home to be with the Lord. I sometimes thought about or dwelt on whether there had been ways to prevent what probably happened.

I will not state that it was God's perfect will for David to go the way He did, but I will say with full conviction that he was ready to meet the Lord and that he is safe in God's arms.

My son suffered with anxiety and also physical pain. He had a bad auto accident at age eighteen that seriously damaged his right leg and ankle. Rods, plates, screws were put in. There was a lot of pain involved in the surgery and recovery. Then a few months later, the plate broke, and surgery was necessary again. All the pain started afresh.

David became addicted to the pain medication and would fight that issue for years to come.

Short version: my son was on multiple prescribed medications.

These medications apparently slowed his respiratory system down. David had a single dose of a pain medication in his system that was not prescribed to him. Someone no doubt gave it to him to help him. The coroner stated his heart stopped.

Even knowing all along what had probably happened, reading the report was so painful. All the tears and pain emerged. Even as I write — I had to take a few days before I could write this down. As much as God has helped me, given me peace, it brings back the troubled times of the heart. The evil one again tried to inject himself into my peace.

Why did it take nine months to get the report? During these nine months' wait, God did a work in my heart. Now Satan thinks he can steal it?
No way, he's too late!

God had lifted me in my emotional pain. I once again knew I needed a song of inspiration. I reached for YouTube. The site knows your history and will pop up suggested songs from that — I have many! The site doesn't know my need today, but God does. The first song that popped up, with no searches initiated by me, was "Going Home to Be with Jesus" by the McGruder's. How good is God?

For those that don't know it, here's one verse.

"I'm going home with Jesus in the twinkling of an eye.

I've made my reservation for a mansion in the sky.

I may not know the moment; I may not know the day.

But I know that I'll be leaving when He calls His church away."

Note:

The next experience will probably be my last entry. I want to close with it. Before I tell it, though, here are a few thoughts. Each and every visitation I have endeavored to share was a mighty experience God blessed me with. I am but one small soul in God's kingdom. His grace, mercy and love are there for any and all to accept. It is simple: pray, ask, believe. He will hear you. The answer will come.

At the conclusion of this next blessed experience, I realized with a deep revelation that God has said, "It's time to remember with joy the good times with David." There will be times of missing him, and human sorrow will remain, but David and the Lord are ready for Dad/Marcus to remember the good times and the blessing reunion day will bring.

God has certainly continued to bless me and provide the strength that only He can give, and even additional special visitation moments.

After the following event, it became very clear to me that I was to put these things down in writing in book form to testify to others.

Since that day, and it has been over a year at this time, my daily thoughts have been focused on these writings. I say daily; however, the emotions of writing caused me days and weeks of pause sometimes.

I go to Las Vegas, NV on business occasionally. Stretching some visits into vacation time is enjoyable for us. We enjoy dining at some very nice restaurants and, of course, some great steakhouses. I took my sons a couple years back. We took in some shows that had a family atmosphere. We also had a fantastic journey into the Grand Canyon, Hoover Dam, Lake Meade, etc. The photo of David that I had put on canvas and hung in our office as a memorial was taken there as he stood on the rim of the Grand Canyon. Yes, he scared me there — so fearless!

I really enjoy the golf in Nevada. Desert courses are unique to me.

On this visit it was just Iris and me. This particular day, I visited an Arnold Palmer designed golf course named Arroyo, located in near- by Henderson, Nevada. Actually, Iris and I had played there a couple of days earlier in our visit. I went back this day to play alone, and Iris took off for some shopping.

The golf course paired me with two other gentlemen, as is customary if the course is getting crowded and tee times are filling up. These were both very nice local members of the course. They both were a few years older than I, retired. They played golf multiple times per week.

Being seniors, they preferred to play from the #4 tee boxes.

When playing alone, I normally play from the #2 tee boxes, and my handicap supports that.

Being a little younger, I felt comfortable asking if they minded if I played from the #3 tee boxes. It would feel arrogant to step back to the #2's; though it's totally proper, I'm a visitor, new to the course, and I am humbled to play a round with two good local members.

They said, "Please do; you are younger!" I smiled, realizing they are in their late sixty's, but I'm sixty-three.

It was a good day for me. I was hitting most fairways. We complimented one another on good shots, as gentlemen golfers do. I was hitting some long tee shots, and they were repeatedly complimentary.

Somewhere about hole eleven or twelve, I hit my longest tee shot of the day. The ball ended up 330 yards from the tee box! There was some roll out, but the carry was long. Golf balls do travel about ten percent farther in this area than back in North Carolina or most areas of the country. The elevation is a few thousand feet higher, so the air is thinner. The ball simply travels farther through thinner atmosphere.

At the age of sixty-three, and not near my physical best from years past, three hundred yards is absolutely the very best I can hope to achieve, and that's when all comes together in my swing correctly. Back home I average 270 yards, and my very best at this time of my life is 290-300 yards.

So, on hole eleven or twelve or whatever it was, add ten percent to 300 yards, and I had the best I am capable of, and that is rare.

I share these particular points about my game so that you better understand the magnitude of what God allowed me to experience today with my son David, coming up.

The special visitation and experience with God and David occurred on hole number sixteen. It will live with me through eternity.

We pulled our golf carts up to the tee boxes on hole number sixteen. It is a par five, 475 yards from the #3 tee box. The golf group ahead of us was still in the fairway awaiting their second shots, as they waited on the group in front of them. We had a few minutes to chat so I got out of my cart and went up to my two playing partners' carts where they sat and waited. We had done a little chatting throughout the day, but very briefly, as we had not had to wait on others before now.

When I first walked up, they once again complimented the drive I had a few holes back, the 330 yarder. It's kind of opened the stage to tell them a story about David that related to conversations we had back home when I had a big drive. However, they knew nothing about David, so I was not inclined to bring it up. We continued the small talk; the kind of conversations new acquaintances have. The normal, "What do you do for a living?" "You here on vacation?" "Are you retired?"

The usual back and forth, and then, "Do you have children?" At first, I was afraid to answer. Answering that question had always brought out emotions and tears desperately held back. I suspected that would never change, as it was always a bubble waiting to burst.

I answered slowly at first. "Yes, I have two boys." I continued, "David is no longer with me. He's gone on to that heavenly dimension." The guys profoundly offered their condolences. I told them how David was most often my golfing buddy, the fun we had, etc. After a few moments of sharing these times, - apparently, I was smiling - they made the comment, "You have great memories — that's good!"

The comment actually startled me. I realized for the first time ever, my initial reaction in talking about David to someone new was joy, and I was talking about the great memories and not the despair.

The tears of missing him are always in my soul, but up to now they always streamed down my cheeks. For the first time ever, I was joyfully talking about my son. They noticed it and commented to me about it, and that realization excited me.

As I took in this, I was smiling, but I was actually shaking... God's presence!

The fairway cleared, and we needed to be up for our shots. As we walked together back to the #3 tee box, one of them again remarked on the long, good previous drive I had a few holes back. It prompted me to tell them a story I just recalled with David.

I had to hurry the story, as I was up for the tee shot.

The first professional golf match I ever attended, many years back, was on the "Seniors Tour," today called "The Champions Tour," in Clemmons, NC. I was close to the tee box when Chi-Chi Rodriguez and Lee Trevino teed off. After Chi-Chi's drive, he commented, "Now that's longer than some people go on vacation!" The crowd roared with laughter.

One day, when I was playing a round with David, I hit a long straight drive, and I quipped that line to David.

Apparently, I had used that line a few times before. David quickly reminded me, "Dad, you say that every time!" I didn't realize it, but I guess I sounded annoyingly repetitive. David wasn't annoyed, though. It was his way of comically saying, "Awe shut up." He was often sarcastically funny.

I was recounting a great memory I had with David to these gentlemen.

With a big smile on my face, I walked up to the tee box and teed up my ball. Instinctively feeling the moment with David, I looked up into the sky and said aloud for my playing partners to hear, "This drive is for my son and the Chi-Chi story!" I hit my drive.

When the golf ball launched, I knew it was something special. The trajectory, how it rocketed off the club face, how it leveled out at the peak of its trajectory and soared.

It literally sounded like a meteor when it whistled away. It blasted down the left-center of the fairway. Both gentlemen shouted, "Now that's a great drive!"

I didn't know how special it was until I reached my ball. Both of my playing partners hit their second shots, and they were still slightly short of my tee shot. I remind you: this is a par 5. Their third shot is in the layup area. My tee shot is in the layup area.

To be clear, this is a desert course; however, it is well irrigated and very well maintained. I won't say the fairways are soft, but the turf is very plush and has a cushion feel under your feet. The rollout of a high trajectory shot is not above normal, ten yards maybe. The terrain is very flat on this hole and the whole course. There was no rollout as a result of a downhill landing.

As I glanced over to them awaiting their shots, the expressions and hand gestures were obvious regarding my tee shot.

"That's an incredible drive, Marcus!" one of them complimented.

I pulled my golf cart over to my golf ball on this par 5 hole. My ball had come to rest completely through the fairway cut. I pulled my laser and shot the yardage to the flag. Ninety-eight yards to the pin! My drive had travelled 377 yards! I all but broke down crying immediately, as I felt David's presence. I felt God's presence again, and the message rang clear in my ears and heart.

"Remember the good times God gave me with David." I will always miss him, but it's time for me to remember the good times — the memories — and testify to others!

People, I cannot hit a golf ball 377 yards. I do not have the physical capability to do that. It is not in my ability on any day, if I'm exceeding my best, to hit a golf ball 377 yards. Even if you back out the ten percent high altitude factor, the number is still 340 yards and limited rollout. I did not accomplish that on my own.

As I backtracked my golf cart to return to the golf cart path, after hitting my ninety-eight yard approach shot to the green, I closely inspected the landscape to see if there was anything, any object, -a sprinkler head, anything - on my golf ball's path that it could have hit to propel it forward more. There was not. The drive was a very straight, left-center of the fairway shot. There was nothing but plush turf in the pathway of my drive. This drive came at a time God was impressing me, and I believe through David's presence as well, that it is time to feel the joyful memories.

My thoughts went back to when I stood on the 16th tee box beside my partners in the moments before. I realize now that I was smiling as I shared David with them and recalled great moments. This was a first. Tears had always come before, in such moments. My first thought when I lasered the flag from the end of my drive position was, God says it's time to remember the joy of

David. I will be with him again when it's my time.

This experience was meant to be. My golfing partners had repeatedly complimented the previous long drive I had a few holes before.

They did so in the golf cart waiting on the 16th. They complimented me one more time as we walked over to the 16th tee box. That last time stirred my mind to tell them the Chi-Chi story. This was all in God's plan. I was supposed to tell that story and make the statement before my shot: "This drive is for my son and the Chi-Chi story." There is no doubt with me that in some way God allowed David to influence the flight of my golf ball on the 16th hole of Arroyo in Henderson, NV. Maybe God allowed David to influence my swing. I don't know how it happened, but I know it was God; it wasn't me. There is 100% certainty that David was present with me this day, and God allowed him to give me this experience. God has brought me such a long way in the last two years. He has saved me!

I love you, Lord! I love you, David!

I'll see you when it's my time.

EPILOGUE

The most difficult time of my life was, and ever remains, losing my son David and the relationship in this life. David going to that Heavenly home before me was simply crushing.

The most wonderful gift I have ever received is the Lord's assurances He has provided me of David's heavenly home and the knowledge of the reunion I will someday have. These gifts I have endeavored to share in this book. These gifts/experiences have granted me the assurance, the knowledge, the undoubted reality that David is with the Lord and indeed has a blessed position and, I believe, responsibilities in the Heavenly realm.

No greater gift can be given or received than the revelation by God that your loved ones are safe and that you will someday share eternity together. These writings are my testimony of God's grace, strengthening me to get through the life on earth He has planned for me. We all are a part of His work, with an eternal promise of glory if we follow his path.

While we are all unique and God knows each and every one of us by name, we form a body of Christ if we choose His path. I believe Calvary solidified my destiny to eternal life and so it will be for those that accept Him.

His grace, mercy, and love reach all mankind if we walk in all we know.

Our Lord is omnipotent. He has mercy on those He chooses to have mercy on. I have truly learned that if I walk by faith in Him, nothing is too hard to bear. He knows my steps before they are taken and has allotted me His grace and mercy if I simply ask and believe. I truly believe there is a way ordained by God that we all must walk. I also have learned by His mercy and grace what is required of me.

I started writing primarily to remind myself of God's assurances when I reached low points and was overcome with pain and sorrow.

Later I realized I must testify of these things. It became a burden on my heart to produce something I could give to those I come in contact with that need spiritual words of encouragement.

I mentioned earlier that if you are an unbeliever, maybe even an atheist, don't waste your time reading. But my most sincere prayer is that I could touch someone's heart that fits that model, to just for a moment question that disbelief. What if you are wrong? Where did that sense of reasoning, those beliefs come from? Was it another unbeliever? Was it science? Who interprets science? I submit that there is more science to suggest there is a higher Being than there is to suggest not. Can you prove there is no God? Who are we?

We are born of flesh and pass on. These bodies decay and return to earth.

I am and, if you believe, you are a child of God; your soul never dies. God put you here for a purpose. I pray you will seek God and fulfill that purpose. The Lord came to us as flesh. He died for our sins. He gave us a choice in serving Him, following His paths, and the reward of eternal life. He provided His presence in our daily lives to carry us through the travails of life. If you desire that presence in your life, fall on your knees and ask. The God of this universe loves you and will answer.

My thanks to God and my token to David is this book, in hopes that it will inspire, strengthen, and inspire your faith, to look diligently to God for that peace only He can provide when such a time as I have experienced should visit you.

May God richly bless and reward your faith!

POSTSCRIPT

Daniel and Jennifer set up a room in their home to honor David, called "The Dave Cave." They created and ordered a banner that would say that. Weeks went by without receiving it. They did some furnishing, much of David's stuff, and forgot the order had not come.

On Daniel's birthday, October 29, 2018, the banner showed up! David's birthday present to Daniel: "The Dave Cave"

Made in the USA
Columbia, SC
07 February 2024

31636461R00072